CURIOUS CRITTERS®
MARINE

DEEPLY CURIOUS

Oceans cover more than seventy percent of the Earth's surface, yet we have explored less than five percent of their waters. Large land animals capture our imaginations daily; strangely, however, few of us know much about the equally, if not more, amazing animals in and around the sea.

This book, the third in the *Curious Critters* series, explores a handful of incredible ocean inhabitants. By gazing upon these unique creatures—and by hearing what they have to say—we may better understand the coasts, reefs, and deep waters of the United States, Canada, and Mexico.

May this book whet your curiosity and these pages become your snorkel, fins, and mask. Dive in! A wet world of wonderful critters awaits you.

For my mother, Judy, who instilled in me a love of nature and literature.

All animals portrayed in this book were handled carefully and not sedated. Some resided at centers dedicated to education, conservation, and rehabilitation. Wild animals were returned safely to their habitats. Thank you to the Alaska SeaLife Center, Bowling Green State University, Maritime Gloucester, Mote Marine Laboratory and Aquarium, Mystic Aquarium, Palm Beach Zoo, Peace River Wildlife Center, Toledo Zoo, and The Turtle Hospital for opportunities to photograph your amazing animals.

Additional Curious Critters: brown pelican, front jacket flap; pencil urchin, page 1; Atlantic mackerel, pages 2–3; smooth lumpsucker, page 32; rose sea star, back jacket flap; gray treefrog and American alligator, jacket back; and lined seahorse, spine.

FitzSimmons, David. Curious Critters Marine / text and photography by David FitzSimmons.

SUMMARY: A variety of animals common to North American seas pose for portraits against a white background while narrating distinctive aspects of their natural histories.

ISBN 978-1-936607-72-3 (hardcover)
1. Marine animals – North America – Juvenile literature. 2. Coastal animals – North America – Juvenile literature.
3. Sea birds – Juvenile literature. 4. Deep sea animals – Juvenile literature. 5. Animals – Juvenile literature.
6. Picture books for children. 7. Nature photography.
QL122.2 .F58 2015
2014911087

First Edition, April 2015
10 9 8 7 6 5 4 3 2
Printed in China by Great Wall Printing Company Limited

SIGMA

All photos in this book were produced with SIGMA lenses. To learn more about the photographic techniques and equipment used in making this book, please visit www.curious-critters.com.

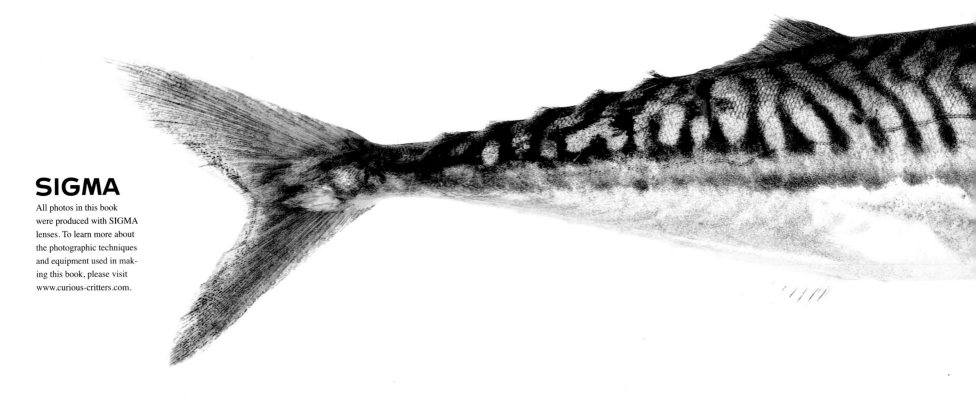

CURIOUS CRITTERS®
MARINE

Text and Photography by
David FitzSimmons

WILD IRIS
PUBLISHING
BELLVILLE, OHIO

ROSEATE SPOONBILL

Forks are fine, but nothing beats a good spoon. I don't mean your simple silverware. I'm talking about my super sensitive spoonbill spoon.

You see, my paddle-shaped bill is covered with nerves. As I wiggle my unique beak back and forth in the water, I can feel small animals hiding in the mud and sand. When I detect fish, shrimp, insect larvae, and other mini morsels, I snap my dipper shut and eat 'em up. Best of all are shrimp. The more I eat, the rosier my feathers become!

The muddy waters of my mangrove are calling. My table is set. Time to use my super spoon!

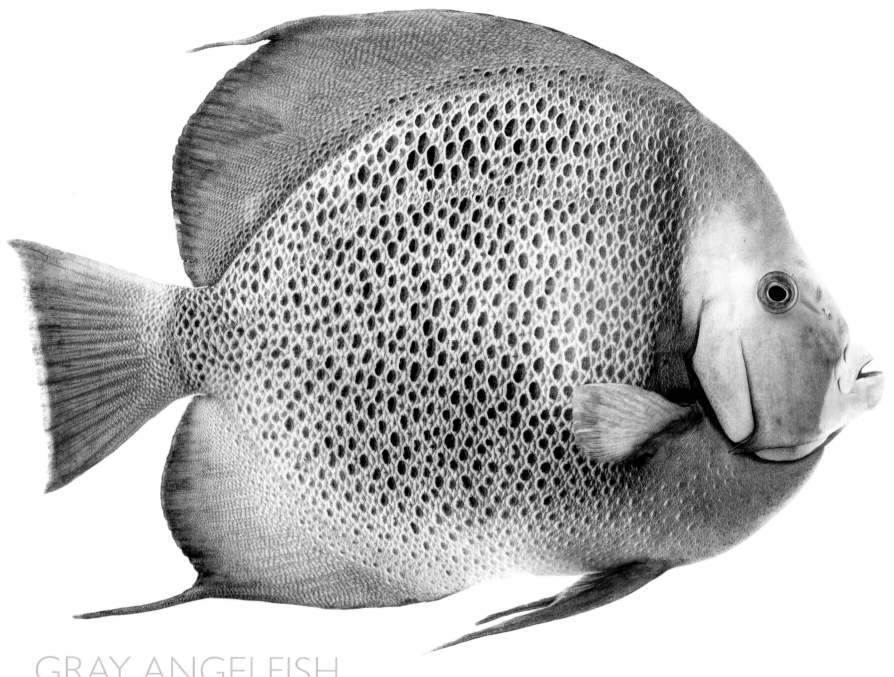

GRAY ANGELFISH

Swim so happily angelfish.
Give your little fins a swish.
Twist and turn within the reef.
Nibble sponges with your teeth.

From the eggs that you will lay
Larvae hatch within one day,
Freely floating in the sea,
Eating plankton hungrily.

Grow so swiftly, little fry,
Find the reef as time goes by.
There you clean off other fish,
Making parasites your dish!

Hide so quickly. Watch your back.
Predatory fish attack.
Flick your body, oh, so fast.
Flip your tail and dart on past.

ATLANTIC HORSESHOE CRAB

Old? You bet! Well, not me. I'm young, but my relatives swam in Earth's seas long before dinosaurs were around. And you don't survive 450 million years without all kinds of tricks—which, thankfully, my ancestors passed along to me.

Take my strong senses, for instance. I'll bet you can spot my two, large compound eyes, but did you know that I actually have nine eyes and that I can see with my tail? I can also feel things with 100,000 tiny pegs covering my body.

How about protection? Well, my hard shell and sharp spikes discourage most predators from attacking me as I scoot along the ocean bottom looking for clams and worms. And, if I get flipped upside down, well, I just use my long tail to help me roll back over, right-side up.

Why, with these old survival tricks, I'll bet my descendents will be around for many years to come!

AMERICAN LOBSTER

Ask any sailor, dock hand, or civilian,
I doubt that they know I am one in two million!
A happy mutation, a change of one gene,
colored me blue, not brown or dark green.

As I grow bigger, I molt my old shell.
A new exoskeleton protects me quite well.
If spotted, however, by cod or by seal,
I'm back to my burrow—no blue lobster meal!

Then out of my hole in the deep of the night,
my antennules smell something—it's seafood delight!
Upraised and all ready, my pincers then grab
delectable dishes, like fish, clam, and crab.

So cobalt and curious by light of the day,
my brilliance makes seafarers readily say,
"Forget pirate treasure and go find for me
a one-in-two-million blue gem of the sea!"

LOGGERHEAD SEA TURTLE

Whew! When I think back to the day I hatched, it makes me tired. With
a hundred of us struggling to get out of our buried nest, sand and flippers
were everywhere! Then I saw the moon reflecting off the ocean. So, I
sprinted to the surf as fast as I could to avoid crabs, snakes, and raccoons.

Hitting the waves felt so good. I dove in and let the undertow pull me
from shore. Then I began swimming. I paddled for two days—*nonstop*—
until I reached a mat of floating sargassum weed. I plan to stay here
for quite a while. There's plenty of food, such as fish eggs,
crab larvae, and the sargassum weed itself. Plus,
I can hide from hungry fish and gulls.

When I'm older, I'll fire up my flippers and
head back toward shore again, but right
now, I think I'll just hang out here
and wait for some lunch to
float toward *me!*

CALIFORNIA SEA CUCUMBER

Comedy night at the Sand Bar featuring C. Cucumber

A crab, a shrimp, and a sea cucumber begin arguing about who feeds best along the ocean bottom.

"Watch this!" says the crab as she scuttles over to a piece of decaying fish lying on a rock. She devours the morsel immediately. "Whoa!" says the shrimp. "You're quite a bottom feeder!"

Not to be outdone, the shrimp eats a worm wiggling in the sand. "Impressive!" the crab exclaims. "You're quite a bottom feeder, too."

"Bah! That's nothing," boasts the sea cucumber. He then pulls water into his rear end, pushes it into his long water lungs, and squirts it back out. The crab and shrimp think it's cool how the sea cucumber breathes with his back end, but they point out, "We were talking about feeding, not breathing."

"I know," insists the sea cucumber. "When I pulled the water—which was filled with algae—into my lungs, I ate the algae with my rear end. I guess that makes me the real *bottom* feeder."

TUFTED PUFFIN

I love getting all dressed up—putting on my best black feathers, brightening up my bill, and growing two feathery plumes—all for my lovely lady. And each year she does the same for me.

You see, during the winter, when we're off on our own, we don't look so glamorous. But, in the spring, we get all spiffed up, meet at our nesting site, and prepare to raise a new chick. First, we dig our cliffside burrow a little deeper. Then my gorgeous gal lays an egg, which we take turns sitting on. Finally, a month and a half later, out comes our cheerful baby.

To keep our hungry one happy, we fly out to sea, where we chase fish underwater. We often catch nine or ten, which we carry home all lined up in our bills. Back at the nest, we feed our little feather ball for about a month and a half, and then one night—*Ta-da!*—our courageous young puffin walks out of the burrow, leaps off the cliff face, and heads out to sea.

I know, such a sudden departure seems kind of sad, but it's okay. My mate and I will soon fly away, too. Then next spring we'll both get back together, all dressed up and ready to raise another beautiful baby.

BLACK SEA BASS

Brrr! Nantucket's nice in the summer, but in the winter, no, thank you! I prefer to head south.

Each year I migrate four hundred miles, seeing amazing things along the way. In October, I head toward the edge of the continental shelf. That's where the water starts to get really deep—*over a mile to the bottom!* In January, staying along the edge of the shelf, I swim southwest to Hudson Canyon. This enormous gorge is teeming with sea life—corals, sponges, anemones, crabs, lobsters, dolphins, whales, and countless fish.

Finally, in March I stop swimming when I reach the waters off the Virginia coast. But, almost as soon as I arrive there, winter starts to let up. So, I speed my way back along the same scenic path to Nantucket, arriving in May for spawning.

HAWAIIAN REEF HERMIT CRAB

Aloha! I'm so glad you could come to my housewarming *luau*.

I'd been looking for a new home for at least a month. Circling around and around the reef, I checked out every open shell I could find. None seemed right, yet I was growing bigger and bigger. Then yesterday, while I was tearing into a piece of decaying fish, I noticed one of my neighbors moving out of this spectacular spiral.

Immediately, I was taken with the trendy notch for my eye stalks, the twirly roof, and the trim of green and red algae. In terms of square feet, it's a perfect fit. I can pull myself back inside comfortably and close the front door with big ol' lefty.

So, start strumming your *ukulele.*
It's time for a *luau!*

CUSHION
SEA STAR

Look at me, a bright sea star,
out beyond the big sand bar.
Crawling in the shallow sea,
tiny tube feet carry me
out to join a galaxy
of sea stars that look like me.

I can smell with my tube feet
lots of food for me to eat,
sponges, worms, and crab larvae,
raked in piles down under me.
Then my stomach, inside out,
eats the food—plus sand, no doubt!

Tough and bendy is my skin.
That's my exoskeleton.
Tiny eyes adorn each arm,
helping me avoid most harm.
If my arms get injured though,
new appendages I grow.

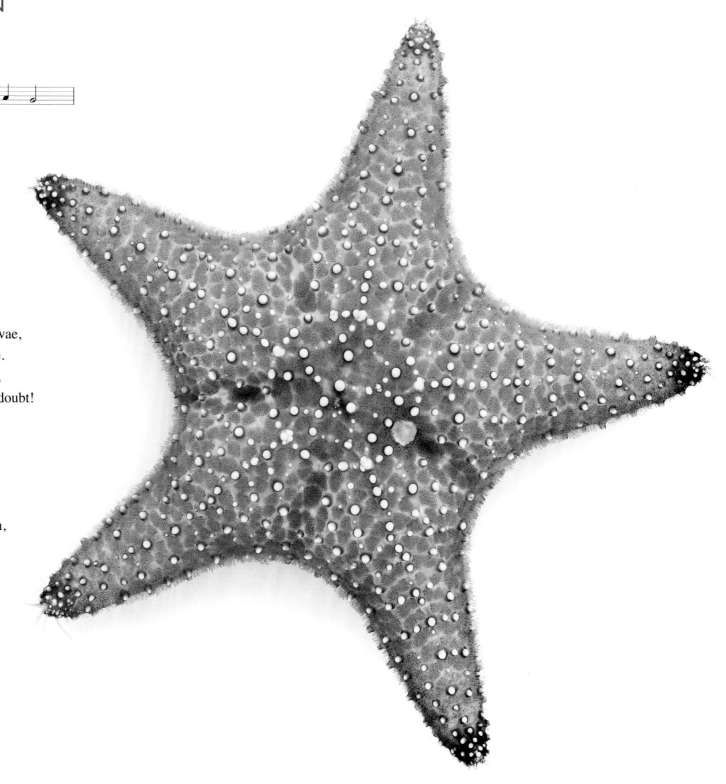

HOODED NUDIBRANCH

I'm quite fashionable for a slug. From my sheer dress to my eye-catching hat, I'm nothing but flair and finesse.

The first rule of gastropod fashion is "Pay attention to your feet." I have found that my "stomach-foot"
looks stunning on green. So, I plant myself on the most fabulous kelp I can find.

Even though my snaily sisters say shells are all the rage, I think gills are more graceful.
So, I wear them all down my back. Quite versatile, I can slip them off if predators attack.

My hat, however, is my most
distinguishing design. Tastefully
trimmed with tentacles, my
fishnet hood is simply fetching.
When prey come my way,
I close my cap and pull
them to my mouth.
Darling, I always
dine in style!

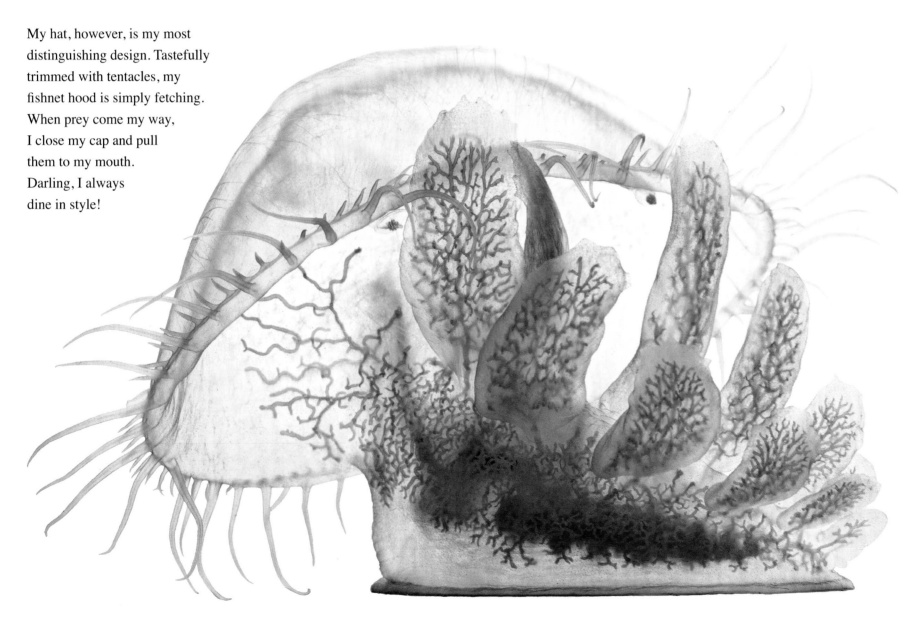

CALICO CRAB

Oh, sure. Whenever there's trash down here, call in the crab. "Come clean it up, garbage guy!" *Grrr!* It never stops.

Rotting redfish, "Where's the rubbish runner?"

Spoiling sponges, "Oh, san-man!"

Atrophying algae, "Jump on it, junk jockey!"

Moldering mollusks, "Yo, Garbo!"

Grrr! Garbo?! That one really gets me. I'm the one down here devouring loads of decaying debris, and nobody applauds my efforts. Without recyclers like me, can you imagine what the ocean would look like? Why, we'd be wallowing in whale waste and covered in crumbling kelp!

RED LIONFISH

I'm the new king of the reef, and I'm coming after you. The thing is, you probably won't even see me. While you are diddling among the corals, sponges, and rocks, I'll be sneaking up on you. My huge, mane-like pectoral fins will camouflage me against the reef and hide my caudal fin back there, stealthily pushing me toward you.

If you happen to notice my approach, don't even think of coming after me. I have venomous spines all along my fins. Go ahead. Try to touch me. You'll be the one roaring in pain.

LINED SEAHORSE

Howdy! Welcome to Seagrass Ranch! We're glad y'all could join us.
How 'bout I show you 'round?

We don't have any set meal times here at the ranch. Just wrap your tail 'round
a plant, stay hidden, and enjoy a seafood smorgasbord of tiny shrimp and other
crustaceans. As little critters swim by, snap out your snout and suck 'em in. *De-lish!*

Sleeping arrangements are pretty simple here, too. Just hitch yourself to some
seagrass and kick back. We'll see y'all at sunrise, bright-eyed and curly-tailed.

Each mornin' we start the day a-dancin'! Grab your partner, hold tails, and swing
'round and 'round. *Yee-haw!*

Finally, y'all be careful. A few predators, like turtles, fish, and rays, lurk 'round
Seagrass Ranch. So, hide yourself well. Change your color a bit to blend in,
and ya'll will be just fine.

Thanks for joinin' us at Seagrass Ranch! Y'all come back now, ya hear?

CANDY
STRIPE
SHRIMP

Most creatures of the ocean
fear the sea anemone.
Its long, stinging tentacles
make it quite an enemy.

How fortunate, however,
that I can call it home.
Throughout its fearsome stingers
each day I freely roam.

And as it calmly eats things,
whatever it deadly taps,
all 'round its li'l mouth parts,
I nibble on its scraps.

And talk about protection!
No hunter catches me.
They fear my faithful bodyguard,
my friend, anemone.

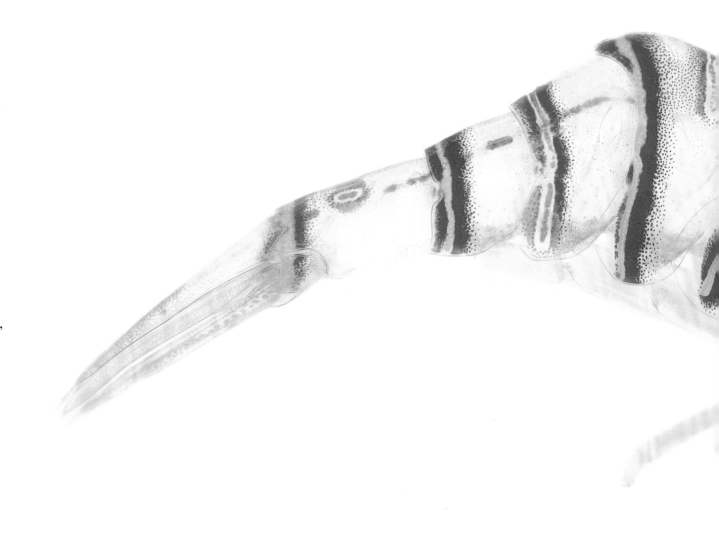

PAINTED FROGFISH

Uh . . . no. I wasn't doing anything. I was just sitting here looking like a sponge and . . .

Well, okay, I might have been wiggling my baited fishing rod above my head. *So what?* It's not like I was trying to lure prey, I mean, uh . . . I certainly wasn't going to . . .

Alright! I admit it. I crept along the bottom using my leg-like pectoral fins to find the perfect spot for fishing, and I did try to camouflage myself like a sponge, and I have been waving my white-tipped dorsal spine all over the place, and, yes, I certainly will gulp down whatever animals try to take my bait!

See? I really wasn't doing anything . . . except *fishing!*

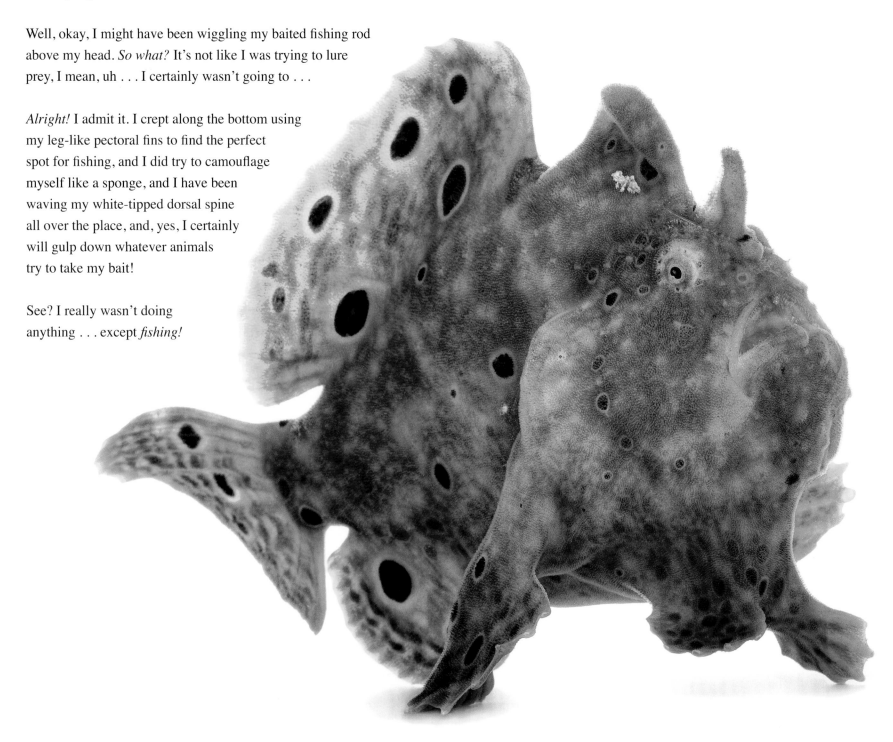

PENCIL URCHIN

Mission Control, Coral Reef here, the Urchin has landed.

We copy you down, Urchin.

Exploring Coral Reef, Mission Control. Tiny tube feet extended, commencing to walk. Daylight here. Headed for protection, searching for a rocky crevice.

Copy that, Urchin. Watch out for predators, especially triggerfish.

Roger, Mission Control. Spines providing some protection, but will seek refuge until nightfall. Exploring the reef, but no crack for hiding, although lots of colorful coral, swaying sponges, and fabulous fishes. All kinds of algae, too, including coralline pink! Extending my horned beak below to commence feeding.

Roger that, Urchin.
Better fill your tank before docking.

Copy that, Mission Control.
This is one small step for Urchin,
one giant reef for sea kind!

DOUBLE-CRESTED CORMORANT

Air, land, water . . . I do it all, but can you guess where I perform best?

Sure, I can fly, but my heavy bones and small flappers make getting airborne a bit of a chore, and I can walk okay, even with my big feet; in the water, however, I'm quick as a fish!

I love to dive, sometimes twenty-five feet deep, and I can stay under for more than a minute. I dip and dodge all along the bottom, looking for food. My wide-webbed feet allow me to push through the water, and my long neck lets me poke my head into all kinds of places where prey can hide—behind rocks, around coral, and into plants.

When I catch small fish, I just gulp 'em down underwater. But, for big fish, I take 'em to the surface, flip 'em in the air, and swallow 'em head first. Yummy!

GIANT PACIFIC OCTOPUS

If you called me an egghead, you'd be correct, but not because of my bulb-shaped mantle. That's my body. I'm an egghead because I'm smart. I'm the most intelligent invertebrate on the planet.

To show off at parties, I solve puzzles, open jars, and find my way through mazes. To survive in the wild, I'm even craftier. I change colors and textures, squeeze through holes the size of your thumb, smell with my suckers, and break into shells with my hard beak, scraping tongue-like radula, and deadly saliva. Pretty *egg*-traordinary, eh?!

UPSIDE-DOWN JELLYFISH

Welcome to my carnivorous garden!

Most jellyfish move freely in the water, but I plant myself on the bottom in a
mangrove forest. There, I cultivate my garden, growing plant-like algae inside
my body. I provide them with nutrients and make sure I sit in the sun all day,
where they can produce food for themselves and for me.

Even though I tend my algae garden well, it doesn't supply
enough food for me to live on. So, I also go fishing. I roll
the edges of my bell in and out, stirring up the water.
As tiny animals come into contact with my arms,
I sting them, and, of course, eat them!

If life gets difficult in the mangrove, I can always
move my meat-eating garden somewhere else.
I just turn right-side up and use my bell to swim
away. But, soon enough, you'll find me back
on the bottom, in the sun, and upside down.

CURIOUS CRITTERS: NATURAL HISTORY

Roseate spoonbills use their broad beaks to find small prey and occasionally plants. The crustaceans these wading birds eat contain reddish pigments called *carotenoids*, which color their feathers pink. The hunting of roseate spoonbills for their feathers, which were used in hats, threatened the species in the nineteenth century, but increased protection has helped their numbers rebound dramatically.

American lobsters are decapods, meaning they have ten legs. The front two are asymmetrical, with a larger pincer, called a *crusher*, for breaking shells and a smaller one for tearing food. Besides long antennae, they sport a pair of down-turned, Y-shaped antennules, covered with over 400 types of smell receptors. American lobsters can shoot plumes of urine from their heads, announcing their presence to rivals or mates.

Tufted puffins, not graceful in the air, are adept at "flying" underwater. After catching a fish, a tufted puffin uses its tongue to hold its catch against barbs found along the top of its mouth. This allows the puffin to catch additional prey. One phenomenal fisher was documented flying back to its nest with sixty fish in its beak!

Gray angelfish are solitary reef dwellers. They grow up to two feet in length. Their tall, thin bodies help them quickly maneuver away from predatory fish and sharks. After hatching from free-floating eggs, larvae feed on plankton and eventually settle onto reefs when reaching about one-half inch in size. Juveniles then feed on algae and parasites found on other fish.

Loggerhead sea turtles are the largest hard-shelled turtles in the world. While they typically grow to have carapaces around three feet long and can weigh up to three hundred pounds, some exceed nine feet and twelve hundred pounds. Beginning their lives in shoreline nests, loggerhead sea turtles swim to sea as hatchlings and then, after about ten years, return to shallower coastal waters.

When not migrating, **black sea bass** are typically found near structures such as reefs, oyster beds, and wrecked ships, where they rest in the water, waiting for crabs, shrimp, fish, and other prey. They can live up to twelve years and grow twenty-four inches long. Black sea bass are typically born female, though many change into males later in life.

Atlantic horseshoe crabs, which are related to spiders and scorpions, may live twenty years or more. As they age, they molt their shells less and less often, increasingly allowing sea life, including algae, barnacles, and various mollusks, to accumulate on their backs. Atlantic horseshoe crabs have blue blood, which can be collected and used for specialized medical purposes.

California sea cucumbers feed on algae, fungi, bacteria, plankton, and other organic matter using a circle of tentacles surrounding their mouth, but they also absorb nutrients through the respiratory trees in their hind end. *Yes, they eat with their rear end!* To avoid being caught by predators, California sea cucumbers can expel their guts and other internal organs and then regrow them later.

Hawaiian reef hermit crabs live in the sand along the edges of reefs. Even though the word *hermit* suggests that these crustaceans are loners, they typically live in groups. As hermit crabs grow, they vacate their shells to move into larger ones, leaving smaller shells behind for others. Sensing danger, these decapods retract their bodies into their shells and close off the entrance with their enlarged left claw.

Cushion sea stars are echinoderms like sea cucumbers and sea urchins. They are the largest of the Atlantic sea stars, growing to twenty inches across. While they normally have five arms, some cushion sea stars occasionally develop more. They feed by turning their stomach inside out to engulf detritus and small organisms, as well as the sediment in which their food is found.

Lined seahorses are not your typical fish. They feed by quickly snapping their heads upward, a motion that instantly draws water and prey into their straw-like snouts. They feed on small plankton, eating continuously throughout the day. And they remain with their mates for life, with the males carrying the pair's eggs in a special pouch until hatching.

During breeding season, **double-crested cormorants** develop feathery crests on both sides of their heads. While most seabirds apply a lot of preen oil to their feathers, making their plumage shed water quite well, double-crested cormorants apply less of it. So, their feathers get wet when diving. Scientists believe this may help them swim better. To dry off, they perch in the sun with their wings spread widely.

Hooded nudibranchs (NOO-duh-branks) are a type of gastropod, a term that means *stomach-foot*. Scented like fruit, hooded nudibranchs attach themselves vertically to kelp stems in groups called *bouquets*. When feeding, they expand their bowl-shaped hoods and wait for small larvae, crustaceans, jellyfish, or fish to enter their traps. Sensing food, they close their hoods, seal the edges with their tentacles, and chow down!

Candy stripe shrimp are found living on and around sea anemones, apparently immune to their stings. They crawl all over the anemones, cleaning up leftovers around their mouths and eating waste released after digestion. Despite the protection afforded by sea anemones, candy stripe shrimp are sometimes preyed upon by a variety of fish, including Pacific halibut.

Giant Pacific octopuses show signs of intelligence once thought to be found only in vertebrates—from physical characteristics, such as lobed brains, to behaviors, such as problem solving. Remarkably, these cephalopods develop their smarts during a short three- to five-year life span! Scientists are studying the varied temperaments of octopuses, investigating whether they have personalities.

Calico crabs are mainly detritivores, eating decaying plants and animals. The colorful carapace on these crustaceans helps them blend in on the sea floor. Often calico crabs have tricolor anemones hitchhiking atop their shells. In this symbiotic relationship, sea anemones benefit from crabs carrying them to food, and crabs benefit from the protection of the anemones' stinging tentacles.

Over time, **painted frogfish** change colors to match their particular habitats. Like other anglerfish, they have a modified dorsal spine that forms a fishing rod, called an *illicium*, and bait, called an *esca*. When animals try to grab the esca, the painted frogfish's jaws reflexively open, greatly expanding the size of the mouth and thereby sucking in both water and prey.

Red lionfish, native to the western Pacific and Indian Oceans, have—thanks to human assistance—invaded coral reefs in the eastern Atlantic Ocean, the Gulf of Mexico, and the Caribbean Sea. While hunting, they blow water at their prey, likely confusing them. When close enough, lionfish strike in the blink of an eye. Venom, found on eighteen of their spines, causes great pain for humans.

Pencil urchins, related to sea stars and sea cucumbers, have bodies or *tests* made of five radially symmetrical parts. From these, ten rows of large, movable spines extend, providing protection. Surrounded by small tube feet, which provide locomotion, is this echinoderm's beak. Its five sharp wedges scrape algae off coral, as well as chew on sponges, barnacles, and dead fish.

Upside-down jellyfish have a symbiotic relationship with algae, both benefiting from living together. Growing the size of a dinner plates, upside-down jellyfish live in groups within mangroves and in the shallow waters of sandy mudflats. All along their eight arms are stinging cells, which stun prey. While other jellies have one central mouth, upside-down jellyfish have hundreds of tiny mouths all over their arms.

CURIOUS CRITTERS
LIFE-SIZE SILHOUETTES

1

6

7

Can you identify the animals?

5

2

8

11

9

4

3

10

How many animals' silhouettes have been reversed? Which ones?

What do the silhouette colors mean?

Answers are on the next page.

GLOSSARY

Algae: plant-like organisms, ranging in size from a single cell to giant sea kelp, that, through photosynthesis, convert sunlight into food; singular, alga.

Bell: the umbrella-shaped portion of a jellyfish to which tentacles are attached.

Carapace: the exoskeleton or hard shell covering the back or part of the back of animals such as turtles, crabs, and lobsters.

Caudal Fin: the skin-covered spines at the back end of a fish used for propulsion; also called the tail fin.

Chelicerate: one of a sub-group of arthropods that includes horseshoe crabs, as well as spiders, scorpions, and ticks.

Cnidarian (ny-DAIR-ee-uhn): one of a group of animals that includes jellyfish, sea anemones, corals, and hydras.

Coral: a marine animal that frequently lives in colonies and produces a hard, chalky skeleton that forms reefs.

Crustacean: one of a group of animals, typically with hard exoskeletons, such as lobsters, crabs, shrimp, and barnacles, as well as smaller organisms, such as copepods and amphipods.

Detritivore: an animal that feeds on detritus or decomposing plant or animal matter, as well as feces.

Echinoderm: one of a group of radially symmetrical marine animals, including sea urchins, sea stars, sea cucumbers, and sand dollars.

Exoskeleton: a hard structure found on the outside of an animal, supporting and protecting its body.

Gastropod: one of a group of animals made up of aquatic and terrestrial snails and slugs; the name derives from the Greek for *stomach (gastro)* and *foot (pod)*.

Gene: a microscopic part of a cell that determines an inherited trait of an organism.

Larva: a juvenile life stage of animals that undergo complete metamorphosis; plural, larvae.

Mangrove: any of a group of tropical evergreen shrubs and trees with stilt-like, intertwining roots and growing in shallow, coastal salt water.

Mollusk: one of a group of animals, often with hard shells, that includes clams, oysters, mussels, scallops, snails, slugs, octopuses, squids, and chiton.

Mutation: a change within a gene that may result in a new characteristic, which occasionally may be beneficial to the organism.

Pectoral Fin: one of the two sets of skin-covered spines on the sides of fish.

Plankton: aquatic organisms that are unable to swim against currents, serving as an important food source for many other organisms; singular, plankter.

Preen Oil: a substance secreted by a gland near a bird's tail and applied with its bill that helps maintain the integrity and waterproof characteristics of its feathers.

Radula: a rasping, tongue-like structure of most mollusks, covered with tiny teeth and used to scrape during feeding.

Reef: a structure submerged in the ocean, often formed by sand, rock, and, in tropical waters, coral.

Sargassum: a type of marine algae, often called seaweed.

Spawn: to deposit eggs in water.

Sponge: a pore-covered animal, often found in large colonies, that pumps water through its body to catch food (plankton), obtain oxygen, and remove waste.

Symbiosis: an often mutually beneficial association between two organisms.

Tentacle: an elongated, flexible, and mobile organ most often used for grasping and feeding, sometimes for touching, tasting, seeing, or smelling.

Tube Foot: one of numerous, moveable projections on echinoderms, such as sea stars, sea urchins, and sea cucumbers, used for moving, feeding, sensing, and breathing.

Water Lung: in sea cucumbers, a respiratory system that includes two tree-shaped breathing structures that absorb oxygen from water sucked into the rear end.

Answer Key to Silhouette Pages: 1. Roseate Spoonbill, 2. California Sea Cucumber, 3. Hawaiian Reef Hermit Crab, 4. Painted Frogfish, 5. Black Sea Bass, 6. Giant Pacific Octopus, 7. Cushion Sea Star, 8. Lined Seahorse, 9. Atlantic Horseshoe Crab, 10. Upside-Down Jellyfish, 11. American Lobster, 12. Tufted Puffin, 13. Calico Crab, 14. Red Lionfish, 15. Hooded Nudibranch, 16. Loggerhead Sea Turtle, 17. Pencil Urchin, 18. Gray Angelfish, 19. Double-Crested Cormorant, 20. Candy Stripe Shrimp.

Four animals' silhouettes have been reversed: American Lobster, California Sea Cucumber, Calico Crab, and Candy Stripe Shrimp.

Silhouette Color Groupings:

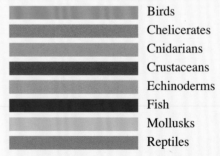

Birds
Chelicerates
Cnidarians
Crustaceans
Echinoderms
Fish
Mollusks
Reptiles

Extra Challenge: Can you identify the Curious Critters not labeled in this book? You can find the answers on page two.

More Curious Critters are on the way! Games, educational resources, and additional photos at *www.curious-critters.com*